Bella's Baby Bird

Written by Avelyn Davidson

Illustrated by Marten Coombe

Pete and Dad were making a new fence. Dad was doing the hammering. Pete was passing him the nails.

"Dad, Dad," cried Pete. "Bella's got a baby bird."

3

"Come here, Bella," called Dad.
"Good girl. Bring it here."

Bella came toward Dad
with the bird in her mouth.

"Drop it, Bella," said Dad.

Bella dropped the bird
in front of Dad.

4

"Is it hurt, Dad?" asked Pete.

"No," said Dad. "But it's frightened."

"What kind of bird is it?"
asked Pete.

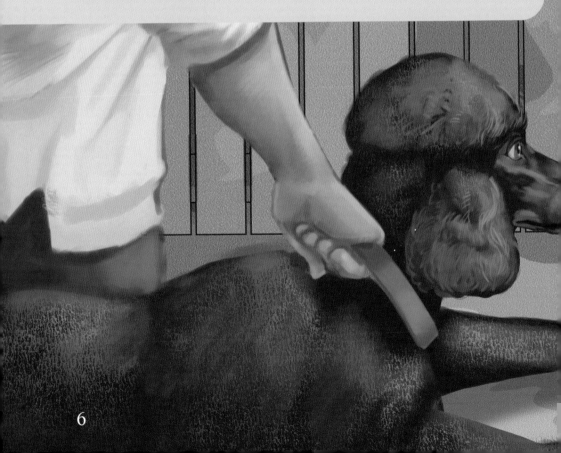

"It's a baby thrush," said Dad.
"It must have been blown out of
its nest in last night's storm.
Pick it up gently, Pete, and we'll
find a safe place for it."

Pete put his hands around
the little bird and picked it up
carefully. Bella licked his hands.

"How can we help it, Dad?"
asked Pete.

"We'll put it under a bush,"
said Dad. "We can watch it while
we work. If its parents are nearby,
they'll come and feed it. You'd
better put Bella inside for a while."

Pete put the baby bird down
gently. "What does a thrush eat?"
he asked Dad.

"Thrushes eat worms, snails,
and insects," said Dad.
"You often see them hopping
on the lawn listening for worms.
Sometimes you see them banging
a snail on the path to crack
its shell."

Pete watched the bird all morning.

"I wish its parents would come," he said. "It must be hungry."

"If its parents don't come today, I'll call the Bird Rescue Center. The Bird Lady will know what to do," said Dad.

13

All afternoon, Pete kept watch over the baby bird. Bella kept watch, too. But the baby bird's parents didn't come.

"Let's bring it inside, Dad," said Pete. "We don't want a cat to get it."

Pete put some dry grass in a box.
When he picked up the baby bird,
it squawked and opened its beak.

"It's hungry," said Dad.

Dad called the Bird Lady
and told her about the
baby thrush.

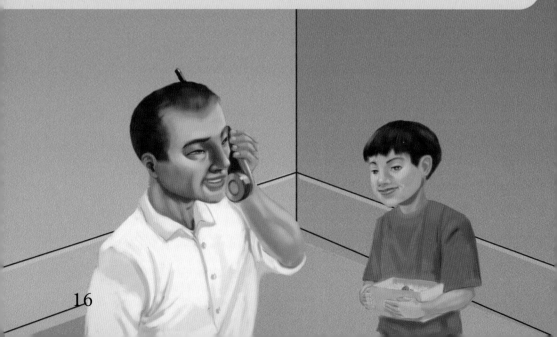

"You must keep it warm,"
she said. "Tonight you could
feed it some hard-boiled egg.
Then tomorrow you can bring
it to the Bird Rescue Center."

Dad showed Pete how to hold the food over the baby bird's beak. Pete dropped the food in. Bella barked at them.

"She wants some, too," laughed Pete.

19

The next morning, Pete and Dad took the baby bird to the Bird Rescue Center. Bella went with them. She barked when the Bird Lady took the baby bird.

"I'll take good care of it, Bella," laughed the Bird Lady.

The Bird Lady showed them around. There were lots of baby birds. There were birds with broken wings and birds with broken legs.

"The sick birds stay here until they are well and can be set free. Your baby bird will stay here until it can fly," the Bird Lady said.

Dad took a photo of the Bird Lady. Then he took a photo of Pete feeding the baby bird.

"Woof! Woof!" barked Bella.

"Let's take Bella's photo, too," laughed Pete. "She found it. It's Bella's baby bird!"